I AM WITH YOU

YEAR B

Scripture Reflections for Couples

Based on the Sunday Readings
Including various Feast Days & Solemnities

A resource written by the *Two in One Flesh*
Christian pro-marriage team

Foreword by Bishop John Hine

Dedication

We dedicate this book to all of our families who have supported us in all our strivings, whether in our primary relationships with each other or with all of our efforts to seek to make known the Good News that we see Sacramental Marriage to be. We also remember with love and gratitude those couples and priests who worked to bring this blessing to us in the first place so very long ago, and those who walked alongside us for so many years. You are always in our hearts, thank you.

First published in the United Kingdom in 2011 by
Two in One Flesh

ISBN 978-0-9571010-0-5

Illustrations by Bernard Jarvis

Cover design by Geoff Poulter
Page design, layout and DTP by Nick Snode / nicksnode@aol.com
Typeset in ITC Goudy Sans Medium 13/16pt
Print Management by Transform Management Ltd, PO Box 2178, Caterham, CR3 6ZT
www.1025transform.co.uk / info@1025transform.co.uk

Contents

Easter Season

Seasons of the Year

Particular Feast Days and Solemnities

Foreword

I am more than happy to recommend this book which will be a most helpful resource to couples who are looking for a way to strengthen their relationship as husband and wife.

Every Sunday we hear the Word of God being read to us at Mass, and, if we are open to it, that Word both nourishes us and challenges us to become gradually more Christ-like as time goes by.

We are familiar with Jesus challenge to his followers: "*This is my command that you should love one another as I have loved you*" (John 15:17) but perhaps we don't take it really seriously because we think that it is so far beyond what we can possibly do.

But married couples frequently show heroic love in their daily self-giving to their spouses and in this way they are truly living their Sacramental vocation of marriage.

Regularly using this book of Scripture reflections based on the Sunday readings could not only nourish couples in their everyday lives, but also help them to focus the light of God's Word on to their relationship and help them to see the 'extraordinary in the ordinary'.

Bishop John Hine

Introduction

Welcome to our book *I AM WITH YOU*. Its purpose is to help married couples relate God's Word in the Sunday readings to their main vocation namely, to love one another as deeply as they can and to share the fruits of that love with any children they may have, their wider family, our Church and society as a whole. Whilst the book is intended to be used as a preparation for, or as a reflection after the appropriate Mass in Cycle B (or Year 2), it can of course also be a benefit at any time that you choose to focus prayerfully on your relationship: simply read the Scripture eadings, consider the given Reflection and (maybe following some discussion) say the prayer together. There are times in our life when our prayer is dominated by intercessions but there are deeper forms of prayer. For an individual, one form is to discover God within oneself; for married couples, there is discovering God in our relationship in every aspect of the 'for better and for worse' times: in the times when we are close to each other and feel full of life, but also those times when one or both of us are hurting, God is always with us. We hope that this book will help you to discover what God is saying to you, just as you are, each time you use it.

The authors

We are four couples and a priest who went on a Catholic weekend for married couples some years back and have been involved in Marriage and Family Life Ministry as well as various other ministries within the Church ever since.

The origins of the book

We came together as a result of our mutual concerns regarding the specific support for marriage in the Church, deciding to meet to explore the distinctive aspects of marriage as a Sacrament and what, if anything, we could contribute towards the conversation. This proved to be an interesting, challenging and enriching experience for us all. It had its difficulties; we came from the North, South, East and West of this lovely country of ours, so getting together wasn't easy. It also took us considerable time in finding some common ground on what we wanted to do, say, or achieve. However, we met at one another's homes over a period of time, usually for a couple of days (invariably over a weekend) two or three times a year. Such gatherings meant not only a deepening of friendships, a lot of hard work and some good laughs, but also a growing sense that we did have something to offer. We decided upon a three pronged strategy: first we sought to determine what we saw to be the needs regarding the current standing of marriage in the Church, then we tried to agree between us what could be done, in a practical sense, to respond to those needs, and thirdly we determined a programme of action based on our conclusions.

Whilst our ideas were still in embryo stage, the Bishops of England and Wales, led by Bishop John Hine, initiated a countrywide consultation on marriage and family life which led to them producing the document, "*Not Easy But Full of Meaning – A Report of the Findings Listening 2004, My Family, My Church*". We appreciated both the initiative and the contents of the document, and were left with a sense of wanting to build upon it to highlight the specific charism and spirituality of, not just family, but marriage itself.

As a result, some years ago, we wrote to the Bishops of England and Wales to share the fruits of our long period of reflection on Matrimonial Spirituality and the need we saw to be clear about the fundamental role of marriage so that it doesn't get subsumed within the over-riding notion of family. We concluded that marital and family spirituality are two distinct and different realities and that, if the focus is family, we are in danger of losing sight of the fact that for children, their parents love for them is first and foremost deeply rooted in their love for each other as a couple. It is this couple relationship which is not only the cornerstone of family life, but is primarily a sacred calling to a unique and unitive kind of love for the couple themselves. It is in witnessing and experiencing this love that children will grow into a fuller understanding of the love of God for all of us.

Within the papers we sent to the Bishops, we made some recommendations on what we thought might enhance the situation. Their overall response was very encouraging and affirming of the work we had done. Heartened by such positive responses, we were inspired to put together a booklet, based on the submission to our Bishops and called it *Two in One Flesh*. It has been well received and continues to be circulated throughout this country and abroad. Now this book *I AM WITH YOU* is yet another way in which we are hoping to build up, support and elevate the value of Christian marriages, in order that couples may deepen their relationship with each other and with God. It has been a labour of love to get it into print, but it has also been a great gift to us all. We hope and trust that it will be a gift to you.

Acknowledgements

This book came from a desire to make the Good News of Marriage known, but without the patience, time, energy, expertise, and sharing of God-given gifts by others, it might never have made it. We acknowledge with the deepest of gratitude the following:

Bernard and Maureen Jarvis – Bernard for the marvellous and original drawings he has so generously given. He gave us the gift of his time to capture the essence of the reflections in a wonderfully humourous and thought-provoking way. Maureen we thank for her gift of time as well as her patient and kind guidance and her initial editing. We also wish to thank Geoff and Gina Poulter – Gina for all her prayerful support, and Geoff for his advice, ideas, ability to play around on the computer which finally gave us our title, plus all the work on matters related to the design of the book. Finally, we want to thank Nick Snode for his professional guidance and kind help in leading us through the final stages of editing and producing the book.

Every blessing from us,

Brian & Maureen Devine (Brentwood Diocese)

Mark & Liz Dutton (Shrewsbury Diocese)

Maurice & Margaret Magee (Plymouth Diocese)

Canon Frank O' Sullivan (Southwark Diocese)

Peter & Maureen Watson (Plymouth Diocese)

Please note that each reflection carries the initials of the authors as follows: B&M, M&L, M&M, FOS and P&M.

First Sunday in Advent

■ Isaiah 63:16-17; 64:1, 3-8 ■ 1 Corinthians 1:3-9 ■ Mark 13:33-37

Thanking God for each other

"*Stay awake for you never know when the time will come... !*" Today's gospel reminds us that we are called to live each day loving those that touch our lives, full of warmth, compassion, forgiveness and joy in each other, especially with our spouse. When we married we made a covenant to love, honour and serve each other. The Gospel calls us to remember that our lives together will not go on for ever and to thank God for the wonderful gift we are to each other, one of the greatest gifts that the Father has given us. Isaiah reminds us, 'You are our Father. We are all the work of your hand.' It is therefore so important that we thank God every day for each other.

M&L

Thanking God for each other.

PRAYER

Lord, from the bottom of my heart I thank you for the wonderful gift of my spouse, for his/her love and all the care and affection they have given me over the years.

Help us never to take each other for granted and help us always to show the depth of our love.

Amen.

Second Sunday of Advent

Isaiah 40:1-5, 9-14 2 Peter 3:8-14 Mark 1:1- 8

Putting each other first

The invitation for us is to be willing to work at removing all the self-centred behaviours and attitudes which are obstacles in our relationship. These prevent each of us from becoming a better husband or a better wife and from putting each other FIRST in our life together.

When we prepare a way for each other we become a little more powerful, brighter, a clearer signpost of the way ahead for each other, our children, our families and the world around us.

In human terms we can point the way to a New Heaven and a New Earth and the days stretch into infinity.

M&M

Putting each other first.

PRAYER

Lord, as the dark days of winter draw around us, guide us along the path which leads to you, through the love we have for each other.

Amen.

Third Sunday of Advent

Isaiah 61:1-2, 10-11 ■ 1 Thessalonians 5:16-24 ■ John 1:6-8, 19-28

Be happy

In seeking to find images to illustrate the joy in the Lord, that he calls the people to experience, Isaiah uses that of a bridegroom wearing his wreath and a bride adorned in her jewels. These images are relatable to everyone. People will usually stop if they see a wedding party, perhaps hoping that some of the excitement and joy of the celebration will spill over into their lives.

Saint Paul urges the people of Thessalonica to be happy at all times because that is what God expects. Do not suppress or hold back; allow the Lord to guide the Spirit working within you, especially welcome the God of peace for peace is what we all long for.

This peace will make us perfect and holy and safe, and then holding on to these gifts, BE HAPPY.

P&M

Be happy!
Allow the Lord to guide the Spirit within you.

PRAYER

Lord, fill us with your Holy Spirit so that we may be freed from fear and anxiety and so be enabled to help bring Good News to the people.

Especially enlighten married couples to be aware of the powerful witness of their sacramental relationship.

Amen.

Fourth Sunday of Advent

2 Samuel 7:1-5, 8-11, 16 · Romans 16: 25-27 · Luke 1:26-38

Listening is a way of loving

In today's readings David, Paul and Mary listened to God's call and were willing to change their plans and their way of life.

Before you were married you wanted to know everything about each other. You listened intently to everything that was said, and you felt loved and cherished as a result. But, with the passage of time, and the pressures of everyday living, the quality of your sharing and especially your listening might have declined. For all of us, there is a constant need to reflect on the quality of our listening, especially to overcome the temptation to butt in. When we listen with our heart and our eyes, as well as our ears, we begin to recognise aspects of our behaviour and our attitudes that we need to change. Listening is a way of loving... and so is willingness to change. Ask yourself this question: When did I last feel listened to by my spouse? And share your answers with each other.

FOS

Listening is a way of loving.

PRAYER

Lord, you gave us one mouth, two eyes, two ears and one heart, help me to listen with my eyes as well as with my ears.

Help me to look into my heart to discover the reasons why I find it difficult to listen, and help me to make the changes that are needed in order to become a better lover.

Amen.

Christmas Day (Midnight Mass)

Isaiah 9:1-7 ■ Titus 2:11-14 ■ Luke 2:1-14

Presents or Presence

Traditionally, Christmas Day is a great family day with lots of fun and loving interactions. However, statistically, it is also among the worst of days for some families and this, in a high percentage of cases, has led couples to the divorce courts. There are many and complex reasons behind such statistics, but the stresses and strains caused by unrealistic expectations regarding presents and family get-togethers and the pressures leading up to the 'big day', must be contributory factors.

We all know that the first Christmas Story provides a very different perspective, with simplicity as its essential ingredient: Mary, Joseph, the journey on the donkey, the baby Jesus, '*the Word made flesh*' in a stable in swaddling clothes, lying in a manger as there was no room for Him elsewhere. Perhaps the most abiding picture we get from the Gospel readings for today is the intimacy of the get-together there in the stable, the Holy Family with the shepherds and their animals, and the unspoken hopes and expectations of the whole world for that peace and joy of God promised to all people of good will.

Maybe the message to us as a couple, trying to do the best for those we love, is to focus as best we can over this Christmas period on being 'present' to each other a little more than giving 'presents', so that Jesus can be born again in our love for one another and all those we care for.

B&M

Focus when we can on 'presence' to each other.

PRAYER

Jesus, you chose to come among us, as one of us, to be truly present to us in our humanity.

The gift that you gave to us was that you became human so that we might become God-like.

Help us today in our striving to be really present to each other and all those that we love.

Amen.

The Holy Family

Ecclesiastes 3:2-6, 12-14 Colossians 3:12-21 Luke 2:22-40

Give way, love gently and offer wise advice

When Mary and Joseph had done everything that the Law of the Lord required, they went back home. We understand that they were good parents to Jesus, but little is said about them as a couple.

Saint Paul is very clear in his exhortations: '*wives, give way to your husbands, as you should in the Lord, husbands, love your wives and treat them with gentleness*'. It would be a mistake to get caught up in the idea of wives having to submit to their husbands without associating it with what Saint Paul has said elsewhere about love. He says, '*husbands love your wives*' and in his letter to the Corinthians he spells out what he means:

> *'Love waits patiently and shows kindness. Love is not jealous, does not brag, and is not puffed up. Love does not seek self-interest, does not get provoked, and does not rejoice at injustice but at integrity.'*

This is an ideal for us all to endeavour to live by. We might easily imagine that Mary and Joseph lived together in this way under the Law of God. It is a good reminder to us as couples that the best environment for our own children is one where we their parents, as wives and husbands, are committed to making the daily decision to love each other over and above everything else. Naturally, from time to time we all fail, but true love is always ready to forgive... Jesus showed us this perfectly.

B&M

Advise each other in all wisdom.

PRAYER

Lord, we pray that the love we know in our hearts for each other may continually grow stronger.

We ask that through your grace we might strive ever harder to show each other patience, kindness and forgiveness.

Amen.

Mary, Mother of God

Numbers 6:22-27 Galatians 4:4-7 Luke 2:16-21

The wonder of who we are called to be

One of the pictures illustrated in this section of Luke's Gospel is of Our Lady beginning to realise what she was called to be when the Angel Gabriel appeared. The impact that the shepherds had, when they described what they had heard the angels saying, led Our Lady to understand in a profound way that she had become the Mother of God.

For many of us, our understanding of what we become when we marry is something we hear at our wedding but we may not fully realise until something happens to bring about a new understanding much later. We hear that our love for each other reflects Jesus' love for His people. We are also told that the intimacy we share with each other reflects the intimate relationship that Jesus wishes to have with all of us. Despite this we often fail to fully grasp the wonder of what we are called to be.

Perhaps this year might be the time for us to work at understanding the ways that we are called to be a sign. Like Mary, we need to treasure the truth of who we are and '*ponder it in our hearts*'.

M&L

Ponder the wonder of who we are.

PRAYER

Lord, please help us to grasp what it means to you and to others when we love each other deeply; when we share things with each other, listen to each other, and give each other our time and energy.

Help us to forgive our own weaknesses and those of our spouse.

Help us to see that we are truly your evangelists.

Amen.

Second Sunday after Christmas

Ecclesiasticus 24:1-2, 8-12 Ephesians 1:3-6, 15-18 John 1:1-18

You have been chosen

Saint Paul says *'You have been chosen'* and Saint John says *'All things have life in him'*. In a marriage, each partner has been personally called to love their spouse in a lifelong relationship. This is not easy to accept. Most of us think that we decided we wanted to get married, we decided to make the commitment. We certainly did it freely but we weren't always aware that we were answering a call. Priests had a call to answer, not us.

Our love comes from God and each of us is called to live out the gift of that love in our marriage, with His help. The fact that God calls us individually means that He has expectations. I am called to bring life to my partner, to understand and forgive. We are called to pray together, to trust in God's presence in our lives, and to share dreams and plans. We choose to live this way, not just for our own sakes or even for the sake of our children, although they are vitally important, but because our love is an essential part of creating the sort of world that God wants. Living like this also enables other people to see a little of what God's love is like.

M&L

You have been chosen.

PRAYER

Lord, please help us to realise that you have called us to live this life together.

We ask you to give us the graces that we need each and every day.

Help us to realise that when we stumble, you suffer with us and that you are present in our joy.

Amen.

The Epiphany of the Lord

Isaiah 60:1-6 Ephesians 3:2-3, 5-6 Matthew 2:1-12

Our love and unity is a sign

"We saw his star as it rose and have come to do him homage"

Today, our Father reveals through His beloved Son Jesus, His eternal plan of salvation for all His people. As a Church we are all invited to celebrate our unity in the birth of the Christ child.

We, as a 'Little Church' rejoice that the manifestation of the Christ child was brought about through the tender love and care of an ordinary married couple! This 'ordinary' couple are made 'extra-ordinary' by the life they bring into the world. As Isaiah says, "*Arise, shine out, for your light has come, the glory of the Lord is rising on you*", and we, in our married love for each other, are bathed in this same light.

When we first married we lived in the hope that we would be together forever and we too would have children to love and care for. Now, in the evening of our married life together we pray as '*...his glory has shone upon us we too have been renewed in his immortal image...*'

Let us ponder on these things so that we, in the unity of our married love, continue to reflect this sign to each other, our children, family and friends.

M&M

A sign of our love for each other.

PRAYER

Lord, let the light that guided the wise men enlighten our marriage, so that we continue to be a shining example of your love for each other and the world.

Amen.

The Baptism of the Lord

■ Isaiah 42:1-4, 6-7 ■ Acts 10:34-38 ■ Mark 1:7-11

My beloved in whom I delight

In our married love-relationships, we are all God's favourite.

Neither one of us is more important than the other. As we reflect upon this profound and uplifting truth, it is important to work hard at all the little things in our married life. These are the things that build each one of us so that we become '*My beloved in whom I delight*'.

M&M

My beloved in whom I delight.

PRAYER

Lord, bless all the little differences that make us a unique couple as we continue our journey to you.

Amen.

Ash Wednesday

Joel 2:12-18 ■ 2 Corinthians 5:20-6:2 ■ Matthew 6:1-6, 16-18

Now is the favourable time

The readings for the Mass on Ash Wednesday bring together three linked themes: *Penitence, Reconciliation and Prayer*.

It may be helpful to consider the impact of these themes on a husband and wife whose relationship is in need of forgiveness, healing and compassion. Penitence requires us to face up to hurtful situations that can arise even in the most loving relationships. Saint Paul, in his letter to the Corinthians, urges us not to delay in seeking or giving forgiveness: '*Now is the favourable time – this is the day of salvation*'. As married couples, we should avoid clinging on to hurts between us; we should also avoid making each other wait for the compassion and healing that is needed. It is important that we never say a casual 'sorry', but genuinely ask each other for forgiveness in the knowledge that it may take time for the hurt between us to be healed. Let us seek to forgive generously in the silence of our hearts as we are asked to give alms in secret.

Married couples, living in a close relationship together, can find problems between them very painful, but this pain can spur them on to resolve their differences. It is hard for a husband and wife,

t Sunday of Lent

esis 9:8-15 ■ 1 Peter 3:18-22 ■ Mark 1:12-15

We hunger for closeness

e readings for today speak essentially of '*WILDERNESS*' and this n be a reality in our relationship at times during the years of our rriage. When God had Noah surrounded by the sea it must have t like a wilderness of waiting and wondering. Jesus too, during s forty days and nights in the desert, might well have questioned t times why '*the Spirit drove him out into the wilderness*'.

here have been many times when we have puzzled over why we re caught up in a 'desert experience'. Those times when we are sorely tempted to just give up on our marriage, as we struggle with the periods when we hunger for a gentle touch or for the return of the closeness in our relationship. Our desert experience might be a long, cold night of wakefulness pondering on the distance that has grown between us and the lack of intimacy and meaningful communication.

Yet, it's only when we look back on such times that we recognise that the Spirit was at work in and through the pain and the loneliness of our emotional separation. The grace of God was there in the yearning and the awareness of the loss we felt. God was

who are accustomed to being close, to mai
with each other. Reconciliation refers to the p
renewal that follows forgiveness. A married c
an example of reconciliation and rebuildin
When forgiveness and reconciliation have bee
with each other, we still need to ask for recor
through prayer. He supports us when we are c
and welcomes us back when we seek forgivenes
Saint Paul refers to the *'Ministry of Reconciliatic*
all to join him in reconciling ourselves to God.

Now is the time.

PRAYER

Lord, help us through those times when our relationship is broken to s
forgiveness and reconciliation with each other and with you.

Amen.

calling us to make a choice for life; to turn away from our stubbornness, self-righteousness and hardness of heart. He was calling us to live the commitments of our Sacrament, and of the covenanted loving lifestyle we had said yes to on the day when we became two in one flesh. This is a choice we know we need to make in an effective way every day of our life together.

B&M

We hunger for closeness.

PRAYER

Lord, bless our efforts this Lent. Help us to deepen our sense of who we are, in you.

Reveal to us, through your Holy Spirit, how best to grow in our love for one another and those you send our way.

Amen.

Second Sunday of Lent

■ Genesis 22:1-2, 9-13, 15-18 ■ Romans 8:31-34 ■ Mark 9:2-10

Free to be ourselves – Wow

The Transfiguration is the story of Jesus revealing himself to his closest friends and how they were struck with awe. He trusted them with Himself.

WOW!

This makes us think of how we have been amazed, time and time again, at each other's generous sensitivity, thoughtfulness and kindness. These have been occasions when we have had the confidence to tell each other about some of the deep feelings that we have and the times when we have shared our deepest, secret hopes and dreams. We recall the days when we have trusted the other not to laugh, argue or object, and the moments when we have been moved to tears with wonder at each other's understanding, caring and love. Wow, what a calling, what a responsibility!

M&L

Wow!

PRAYER

Lord, please help me to create the opportunities and atmosphere for us to be open with each other and help me to appreciate deeply the wonderful person my spouse is and affirm him / her.

Help us behave in such a way with each other that every one that we meet is helped to experience the beauty of the gift that they themselves are.

Amen.

Third Sunday of Lent

■ Exodus 20:1-17 ■ 1 Corinthians 1:22-25 ■ John 2:13-25

Overturning attitudes that are a barrier to intimacy

As today's Scripture reminds us, God's giving of Himself through Jesus seemed to some like complete and utter foolishness.

When Jesus drives out people selling cattle, and currency exchangers who have cluttered up the Temple, He removes the obstacles which have become distractions preventing His people from fully entering into the presence of God in the Temple Sanctuary.

Here, now, today, is another opportunity for us, as husband and wife, to recognise those attitudes and behaviours which have grown up between us, getting in the way of our relationship together as a couple; that '*sanctuary of oneness*' we hoped and prayed for on our wedding day.

Let us tell each other again, as we did on our wedding day that "*your dreams are my dreams*" and "*I place my dreams into your hands – completely.*"

Then we can experience again that this 'foolish' total giving and receiving is, in the words of the psalmist: "*...more to be desired than gold, than the purest of gold and sweeter than honey from the comb.*"

M&M

Overturning those selfish attitudes that are a barrier to a deeper intimacy.

PRAYER

Lord, as we renew again the temple of our love for each other, grant us the unity that comes from overturning those selfish attitudes that are a barrier to a deeper intimacy with each other and with you.

Amen.

Fourth Sunday of Lent

2 Chronicles 36:14-16, 19-23 Ephesians 2:4-10 John 3:14-21

Saved by grace and called to be a sign

In his letter to the Ephesians, Saint Paul reminds us that God loves us with such merciful generosity that even when we were dead to sin He brought us to life in Christ. Paul also reminds us that this new life is a free gift, not a reward for anything we have done. Our new life is not something that we can earn through good works. Yet this does not mean that we are not called to do them, such as acts of kindness, because these are an essential part of our Christian life. What the reading tells us is that the doing of such works alone does not mean that we merit the grace that is poured out upon us.

One particular way that we married couples can engage in 'good works' is by being a witness to others of the grace that God pours out upon us. In our day-to-day demonstration of our love for each other we can be a model of the love-relationship that God invites us to experience with Him. This witness can be given as a gift to others in simple ways that flow from our married relationship. One way is by choosing to speak of 'our children' rather than 'my children'. Another is by asking to be chosen together to be responsible for ministries in the parish, such as reading the Scriptures, taking part in the offertory procession or simply taking up the collection. All these speak silently to others of a husband and wife's desire to be seen as a couple who love each other. 'Actions' such as this can be particular 'good works' that are freely gifted to our parish family without thought of reward. God's unconditional gift of grace is manifested to us all in a similar way.

P&M

A special sign of God's presence in the modern world.

PRAYER

Lord, help us to bring the gifts of our relationship to our brothers and sisters in Christ.

Amen.

Fifth Sunday of Lent

Jeremiah 31:31-34 Hebrews 5:7-9 John 12:20-33

Unconditional love

Marriage relationships rarely run smoothly, at least that certainly is our experience. There is always a need to give and take. Sometimes it can seem like 'I' am always giving whilst 'you' are doing all the taking! Yet, we know that love is called to be unconditional, '*never counting the cost*'. Indeed, have we not been told that marriage is not about living a lifestyle balance of 50/50 but of both partners giving one hundred per cent?

Jesus gave Himself totally and that is what we are called to do as married couples. This involves a life-long journey of learning to be like Him, in all things and in every way. We could think of our lives together as a 'living laboratory', where all the efforts we make to discover the 'perfection' of how best to love each other in our marriage, are like another experiment to add to the hundreds or thousands that we have already tried!

We are reminded by John in today's Gospel reading that a rich harvest is only possible when a single wheat grain falls on the ground and dies, so it is with every loving effort, trial and tribulation. They are all ways of 'dying' to a life-style that is contrary to what God is calling us to.

B&M

Love is called to be unconditional.

PRAYER

Lord, help us to hear your voice more clearly in our marriage.

Give us the grace to make the choices that bring life to our relationship.

Help us to resent less and to praise more, to let go of small anxieties and rejoice in our uniqueness.

Amen.

Sixth Sunday of Lent

Palm Sunday (The Lord's Passion)

■ Isaiah 50:4-7 ■ Philippians 2:6-11 ■ Mark 14:1-15, 47

Valuable time together – prime time

In today's Gospel reading, before Mark tells us about Jesus' passion, there is the story of how a woman poured an expensive ointment over Jesus' head. When she was criticised for the waste, Jesus said, *"You have the poor with you always, and you can be kind to them whenever you wish, but you will not always have me".*

This reminds us that our time together is limited and therefore it is very precious. So often we are so absorbed by our own activities and priorities that we do not take or make opportunities to spend valuable time together; time to share our thoughts and feelings, to listen, to ask forgiveness and show sensitivity to each other, to hug, or to show affection, and these opportunities are then lost forever.

M&M

Prime time together.

PRAYER

Lord, help us to recognise how precious the time is that we have together. Help us to take every opportunity we have to communicate our love for each other and to grow closer.

Amen.

Easter Sunday

■ Acts of the Apostles 10:34, 37-43 ■ Colossians 3:1-4 ■ John 20:1-9

Be open and honest with each other

In the renewal of our Baptismal promises as members of the Church, we can reflect on our own promise to be a 'Little Church' for each other, our children and our wider family.

Let us remember that the vows we made on our wedding day are a continuing promise for each of us to always be honest and open, thereby preventing anything from blocking our relationship.

Help us to remember that when we make the giving and receiving of forgiveness to each other a vital part of our communication, even the most difficult of problems separating us will be 'rolled away'.

On a day like today, as we ponder the Scripture readings, we too are amazed at the depth of love that God our Father has for each of us. So let us not be afraid either, but take courage in the love we have as we continue our life's journey together.

M&M

Always be open and honest with each other.

PRAYER

Lord, to the amazement and delight of the Apostles, you raised your beloved Son to a new life, with and in you.

Bless us so that we continue to amaze and enrich each other in our married life.

Let us become, more and more, a sign of your continuing resurrection and new life in each other for the sake of our Church.

Amen.

Second Sunday of Easter

Acts of the Apostles 4:32-35 ■ 1 John 5:1-6 ■ John 20:19-31

Doubt no longer

In our married lives it sometimes happens that we are called on to believe something that our spouse has told us even though we find it difficult. Sometimes we are asked to trust our spouse implicitly despite the doubts that plague us.

Suppose we are driving to the airport to go on holiday and one of us gets worried as to whether we have packed the passports. Our spouse reassures us "Don't worry I'm sure we did," but the doubt remains and in the end we are faced with two choices: either stop the car and insist on unpacking bags, risking missing our flight, or trust our spouse's reassurance and continue our journey. If the passports are found can we resist saying "There you are, I told you so." If they are not found can we then forgive the person whose responsibility it was to pack them? Can we trust in our partner's belief that they really thought that the passports had been packed?

Thomas had to see proof of Jesus' wounds before he could believe. Maybe the possibility that Jesus was alive was so overwhelming that he couldn't 'get his head around it.' But Jesus said "*Happy are those who have not seen and yet believe.*" He also said "*Doubt no longer but believe.*" It's important for us to practice trusting our spouse and training ourselves to decide to trust.

P&M

Doubt no longer.

PRAYER

Lord, teach us to trust in you, even when it seems hard to do so.

Help us to remember that to you all things are possible and that if we place ourselves in your loving hands, in time, all will be well.

Amen.

Third Sunday of Easter

■ Acts of the Apostles 3:13-15, 17-19 ■ 1 John 2:1-5 ■ Luke 24:35-48

Finding strength to carry on

It is difficult for us to imagine the feelings of the Apostles after witnessing the death of Jesus. For some of them it seemed that it was all over.

So when Jesus appeared to the Apostles in the Upper Room after his resurrection '*Their joy was so great that they still could not believe it, and they stood there dumbfounded*'. On at least three occasions Jesus had said that He would rise from the dead, but the Apostles had no idea what a resurrected body would look like. Jesus appears and asks for something to eat and He is given a piece of grilled fish. The Apostles still found it difficult to take it in. He told them "*This is what I told you while I was still with you, that everything written about me in the Law of Moses, in the Prophets and the Psalms, has to be fulfilled.*"

There are times in your life as couples when the demands of work, concerns about money and care of the children, leave you despondent and anxious about the future. In times like these you need to remind yourselves of the words of Jesus: "*Come to me all you who labour and are overburdened and I will give you rest.*"

When you take time out as a couple to clarify issues and hand everything over to the Lord, you will find things look different. Your spirits are lifted and you are raised up and find the strength to carry on.

FOS

We find the strength to carry on.

PRAYER

Lord, there are times when our cares and concerns so overwhelm us that we lose sight of our love for each other, and even lose sight of you.

Give us the wisdom we need to keep everything in perspective.

Help us never to lose sight of your love for us and your desire to be with us in all the circumstances of our lives.

Amen.

Fourth Sunday of Easter

Acts of the Apostles 4:8-12 ■ 1 John 3:1-2 ■ John 10:11-18

We lay down our lives, we go beyond...

The Gospel this week is usually developed to highlight the ordained priesthood and how being a good shepherd is one of the primary functions and responsibilities of the priestly vocation. Yet, Jesus is also speaking to us and calling us as couples today. Couples who have been blessed with children could relate it to the 'shepherding' of their children: '*I know my own and my own know me*'. No matter how crowded a place may be, our children can recognise our voices and we know theirs! In addition, shepherding for all Christians refers to our own 'priesthood of the people' inherent through our Baptism.

There are deep truths and challenges that Jesus puts before us as married couples in John's Gospel. Jesus speaks of '*laying down His life...of his own free will*'. In a sense, as a married couple, both of us made such a vow, to lay down our lives for one another; it was our own free will to do this. How hard this can be at times when this vow requires us to listen, submit, to lay aside our superiorities, our sense of being right, our selfish motivations; where are our choices then? When we are filled with negative attitudes and dispositions it is almost impossible to make the choice to put our spouse first. Underpinning the Gospel is Jesus' message of unity – '*there will only be one flock and one shepherd'*. Fundamentally, our Sacrament of marriage requires us to live in a way that bears witness to this call to unity, to go beyond personal prejudices and preconceived ideas, to find common ground; to love one another as He loved us!

B&M

To go beyond.

PRAYER

Lord, thank you for laying down your life for us.

Help me today to look anew at my commitment to my beloved and to remember that I freely chose to love him/her through thick and thin.

Give me the grace to say 'yes' and 'I do' today.

Amen.

Fifth Sunday of Easter

Acts of the Apostles 9:26-31 ■ 1 John 3:18-24 ■ John 15:1-8

Listening and discerning together

One of the poignant pieces of today's Gospel is when Our Lord says *'I am the vine and you are the branches. Whoever remains in me, with me in him, bears fruit in plenty; for cut off from me you can do nothing.'* So often we dream how we would like our Church to be and rush into action without taking the time to pray, listen and discern.

We often become disillusioned when our activities do not seem to bear fruit. Closely related to listening to Our Lord is the way we listen to each other and that needs time to talk, to hear each other's point of view, to pray and discern together. So often Our Lord speaks to us through our spouse and we are reminded of the saying 'The closer we are to each other, the closer we are to God'.

M&L

Time to pray, listen and discern.

PRAYER

Lord, we thank you for the times when you give us ideas and enthusiasm.

Help us always to take the time and have the openness to listen to you and to each other in order to discern what you would really like us to do.

Amen.

Sixth Sunday of Easter

Acts of the Apostles 10:25-26, 34-35, 44-48
I John 4:7-10 John 15:9-17

Called to give our lives to each other

With His demand that we love one another as He loves us, Jesus spells out God's plan for Marriage.

As husband and wife we are called to give our lives to each other as completely as we are able. Then we are asked to reflect back that giving, as a sign to our children, family and friends.

As we ponder on the powerful imagery in Peter's visit to Cornelius, we are reminded that we are all capable of superior attitudes in our behaviour towards one another. It's the little, everyday things which often lead to distances and a lack of involvement with each other, for example, having attitudes of 'His' and 'Hers', 'Mine' and 'Yours' rather than 'Ours'.

As we continue our reflection on the Gospel message and Peter's visit to the household of Cornelius, we are reminded that we are all the '*Beloved of God Our Father*'.

God has no favourites. He loves each one of us with a power and depth we find hard to comprehend. Our mission in life is to reflect that love to each other continually and to all those around us, in all things and in every way.

M&M

To give our lives and to reflect that giving to our children.

PRAYER

Lord, help us to continually see the beauty which first attracted us to each other.

Help us to love and cherish the differences and to continue celebrating, with joy, our unique role as a couple.

Amen.

Seventh Sunday of Easter
The Ascension

■ Acts of the Apostles 1:15-17, 20-26 ■ 1 John 4:11-16
■ John 17:11-19

Striving for unity requires forgiveness

Following the death of Judas, Peter addressed the one hundred and twenty 'brothers' who made up the congregation, stating the qualifications necessary for a successor to Judas: '*Someone who has been with Jesus and us from the time when John was baptising until the day of Jesus' Ascension*'. Having prayed for God's guidance they chose Matthias to take the place of Judas.

As Jesus is leaving His disciples He prays that the Father will protect them from '*the evil one*' and He consecrates his followers '*in the truth*', so that they would remain united as they continued the work that He had begun. Sadly, division soon developed and has continued to do so until the present time. In the past hundred years the movement towards closer unity between all Christians has gathered momentum. Pope Benedict, following the example of several recent Popes, is making strenuous efforts to draw Christians together.

We, as couples, are very aware of the fact that sometimes, despite our desire to remain close, it is sometimes impossible to resolve conflicts about particular issues. We need the help of the Holy

Spirit, who Jesus says '*lives in us*', to prevent opposing views from driving us further and further apart. Forgiveness and compromise might be necessary. What Christian groups often say about relationships among themselves also applies to couples: '*There is nothing more important than what we have in common*'.

P&M

Giving and receiving forgiveness of each other.

PRAYER

Lord, help us to continue to be open and honest in sharing with each other our thoughts and feelings, especially about matters that threaten the unity of our relationship.

Give us the wisdom and compassion we need in our efforts to resolve issues.

Amen.

Pentecost

■ Acts of the Apostles 2:1-11 ■ 1 Corinthians 12:3-7, 12-13
■ John 20:19-23

Differences add richness

At the Feast of Pentecost the Jews celebrated the giving of the Ten Commandments on Mount Sinai and the Covenant that God had made with the Jewish People. At the time of Jesus the Jews had been scattered around the cities of the Mediterranean but they had a strong sense of 'Corporate Identity'. Saint Paul saw the Church as also having a corporate identity. The 'Body of Christ' is made up of people, each with his or her unique identity and talents, and these people are the 'living cells' of the Church. Their different skills and abilities all contribute to the common task of bringing the Good News to the world.

The differences between you as a married couple may have become very evident in the early years of your marriage, and you are still discovering in various ways how different you are from your spouse. These differences can give added richness to your relationship, widening your interests, your horizons. When you share your faith experience with others the differences between you can also be of mutual benefit.

FOS

Added richness – widening horizons.

PRAYER

Lord, on this feast of the Holy Spirit, the Spirit of Love, we give thanks for the blessings that our 'differences' have brought to our relationship.

May the Holy Spirit help each of us discover and use our unique gifts so that they continue to enrich our relationship.

May these gifts also enable us to play our part as individuals and as couples in the life and mission of your Church.

Amen.

Second Sunday in Ordinary Time

■ 1 Samuel 3:3-10, 19 ■ 1 Corinthians 6:13-15, 17-20 ■ John 1:35-42

Welcomed in his name

Today's Gospel readings recount the first meeting of Jesus with some of the men chosen to become apostles: John and two disciples and then Andrew and Simon Peter. They probably did not realise what an important meeting this was but nevertheless they were obviously attracted to Jesus and wanted to spend time with him.

It is interesting to see that when Jesus asked them what they wanted of him, of all the questions they could have put to him, they chose to ask "*Rabbi, where do you live?*" As always Jesus' response was direct, "*Come and see,*" and they went to see where Jesus lived and stayed with him for the rest of the day.

What is not included in John's account is where Jesus was living at this time, although we tend to assume that it was his family home, so that perhaps Mary returning from a shopping trip would have found five or six strange men filling *her house*. No doubt she welcomed them in her Son's name, fed them and saw to their needs. So the stability of a family home might have provided the vital setting for Jesus to begin his mission.

We too recognise that the home environment we provide can be an important gift in spreading the Gospel to others.

P&M

No doubt she welcomed them in her Son's name.

PRAYER

Lord, may we make our home a place of peace and welcome as we seek to live out our calling as members of the Body of Christ.

Amen.

Third Sunday in Ordinary Time

Jonah 3:1-5, 10 ■ 1 Corinthians 7:29-31 ■ Mark 1:14-20

Spreading the Kingdom of God through our marriages

When Jonah was called by God to preach repentance to the people of Nineveh, at first he tried to escape from the demands on him that God's call would involve. Once he accepted this mission he faithfully carried out the task and, as a result, the people repented and God relented of his intention to destroy the city.

Mark tells us that Jesus leaves for Galilee, having been empowered by the Holy Spirit at His baptism in the Jordan. He begins His mission and starts to proclaim the Good News of the Kingdom of God calling people to '*repent and believe in the Good News*'. He then calls Simon Peter, Andrew, James and John and promises to '*make them fishers of men.*' What they made of this call at the time we are not told. Things seem to have finally fallen into place for them when, having risen from the dead, Jesus '*opened the scriptures for them*' to show them how what was written there was pointing to His coming, His saving work and His resurrection.

We are called by our Baptism to be followers of Jesus, called to play our part in Jesus' work of spreading the Kingdom of God. You need to keep opening your hearts to God's love, so that He may reign there as you live your lives as a married couple.

FOS

Spreading the Kingdom of God through our marriages.

PRAYER

Lord, mindful of your love, your goodness and mercy to us as a couple, help us to keep to the path you have called us to follow as we journey together.

Help us to show our desire and to resolve to follow our call as a couple to 'make your kingdom come' by our detachment from worldly values, and our openness to the needs of others.

Amen.

Fourth Sunday in Ordinary Time

Deuteronomy 18:15-20 ■ I Corinthians 7:32-35 ■ Mark 1:21-28

Evangelisation through our Sacrament

At first glance, what Saint Paul is saying in his letter to the Corinthians in the readings this Sunday seems to infer that a deeper spirituality is likely to be found among single men and women. Yet we know that Paul has a great appreciation of the spirituality of the married state, evidenced in his letter to the Ephesians, where he speaks of '*the profound mystery*' of marriage and compares it to the relationship between Christ and the Church (Eph. 5:32).

There is clearly wisdom in all Paul had to write and, whilst it might be obvious that the single life offers greater freedom to devote one's life to the Lord's affairs, we must be careful in our marriages not to assume that these affairs of Jesus are nothing to do with us. Indeed, the Lord is at the very centre of our love for one another and, together with the Spirit, is constantly calling us to His work, and providing the grace we need to keep up with the ongoing outreach and evangelisation possible in and through our Sacrament.

In the Gospel, Jesus is seen to dispel the unclean spirit from within a man who was perhaps unaware of the negativity of this spirit or, if aware, was unable to cleanse himself of it. We too may have a spirit that prevents us from seeing our own goodness or the authority we inherently have through our life now **in** Christ, wherein, as married couples, we can daily witness to his love abiding through us, with us and in us.

B&M

Ongoing outreach and evangelisation through our Sacrament.

PRAYER

Lord, be with us today as we seek to love as you have loved, to love each other, not with a spirit of timidity, but with a wholehearted 'yes', not counting the cost but counting on you to provide us with all the graces that we will need.

Amen.

Fifth Sunday in Ordinary Time

Job 7:1-4, 6-7 ■ 1 Corinthians 9:16-19, 22-23 ■ Mark 1:29-39

Making the time to talk and to listen

One of the striking aspects of Jesus' behaviour as described in Mark's Gospel today is the way that, in the middle of a very hectic period of curing the sick and preaching, He got up long before dawn and went to a lonely place to pray.

Just as it was important for Jesus to spend time with His Father in the peace and quiet of the hills, it is important that, as well as spending time in prayer as a couple, we make time to communicate with each other when we are not tired; a time to talk, to listen, to share with each other things that have happened in our day, and look at some of the feelings and thoughts that arise from what we share. If we do not make this time, it is easy to lose sight of each other and as a direct result find that we are misunderstanding what we hear.

If we are not careful, we can become frustrated with our relationship and resort to other ways of finding satisfaction in our lives. It's very important that we try to do something every week that is a simple celebration of the love we have for each other.

M&L

Time to talk, to listen, to share.

PRAYER

Lord, help us to appreciate the importance of spending quality time with each other as well as with you.

Help us never to lose sight of how special our spouse is and may we always make time to celebrate our love together.

Amen.

Sixth Sunday in Ordinary Time

■ Leviticus 13:1-2, 45-46 ■ 1 Corinthians 10:31 – 11:1 ■ Mark 1:40-45

From loneliness to listening with the heart

Today's reflection might remind us that from time to time we can all experience a sense of isolation, separation, even loneliness in our relationship as a married couple. Living in our modern world can lead to us taking each other for granted, which in turn can lead to loneliness. As a result we can find ourselves at odds, separated in spirit from each other.

But the Lord always wants to heal us. If we acknowledge to each other that this state of affairs can occur from time to time, then we are already on our way to healing. When the Leper said to Jesus "If you wanted to you could cure me" Jesus replied, "*Of course I want to!*". God's love for us has made this healing power real and possible in our relationship.

Through the power of the love we have for each other, '*if we want to*', we can lift and encourage each other when one is low and dispirited. We have the power to heal and strengthen each other through a caring touch and a tender kiss.

To paraphrase Saint Paul, *'I am not anxious for my own advantage but for the advantage of others'. 'Your concerns and anxieties are my concerns and anxieties*". In truly listening to each other with the heart, we are, each of us, rebuilt and nourished to love ever more deeply.

M&M

Truly listening to each other with the heart.

PRAYER

Lord, help us to listen to each other and to you, so that we are continually strengthened in our journey through our life together.

Amen.

Seventh Sunday in Ordinary Time

Isaiah 43:18-19, 21-22, 24-25 ■ 2 Corinthians 1:18-22 ■ Mark 2:1-12

The Lord forgives our sins, so let us forget past issues

The world we live in today is full of people who are burdened with self-inflicted guilt. Perhaps the worst, most pernicious result of this guilt is that it can cut the person off from those who love them and want nothing more than to be allowed to give loving help when difficulties arise. The intimacy of the married relationship means that it is often there that guilt is most painfully present.

However, Isaiah reminds us that the Lord has condemned this habit of dwelling on past issues *"I it is, I it is who must blot out everything and not remember your sins."* Sometimes it is thought that this passage calls on people in a relationship to 'come clean' about every transgression. Yet doing this can lead to dredging up past issues that are best forgotten. The closeness that should be present in the relationship between husband and wife, may lead to the sharing of past issues in the mistaken idea that this will deepen the loving trust between them.

Isaiah tells us that dwelling in past issues only serves to trouble the Lord. So what are we to do when past issues rise up and bother us? One answer is to turn to someone whom you trust, (possibly a priest), who is not involved in the problem and who can help you to look at the matter with fresh eyes and seek the Lord's help in blotting out the pain and guilt of the past.

P&M

The lesson is to recognise the beautiful human qualities we bring to each other.
- Forget past issues -

PRAYER

Lord, help us to give up dwelling on past issues and let you take our burdens and transgressions and blot them out.

Amen.

Eighth Sunday in Ordinary Time

Hosea 2:16-17, 21-22 ■ 2 Corinthians 3:1-6 ■ Mark 2:18-22

You are a love letter from Christ

The Scriptures are often called a 'Love Letter' telling the story of the ups and downs of God's love relationship with humanity. Speaking through Hosea, the prophet of His love, God tells the Jewish people that their time in exile in Babylon was a time of testing. Despite their unfaithfulness, HIS faithfulness to the Covenant has not changed. They will once again come to know the love of the Lord.

Psalm 102 reminds us of God's everlasting Fatherly, compassionate, merciful and forgiving love. *'As far as the east is from the west, so far does he remove our sins'*.

Paul describes the Christians in Corinth as *'a letter from Christ drawn up by us'*. He says that it was not written by us, but by a Covenant with the Spirit of the living God written *'on the tablets of your living hearts'*.

The 'Love Letter' theme recurs in the Gospel passage in which Jesus, the 'Bridegroom', tells his followers that when the Bridegroom is no longer with them, *'the bridegroom's attendants'*, the Apostles and you as couples, will go out to the whole world with the 'new wine' containing the Good News of God's faithful, unconditional love for the human race, shown above all on the Cross. You are called to be a reflection, to 'mirror' the faithfulness of God's love for the human race. The help you receive through your Sacrament of Marriage and through the Eucharist enables you to take on this responsibility.

FOS

A love letter written on the tablets of your hearts.

PRAYER

Lord, we acknowledge with sadness that each of us has been at times unfaithful to the covenant commitment we made on the day of our marriage.

Thank you for the compassion, mercy and forgiveness you have shown us, and have enabled us to show each other.

Through the guidance we receive through the Scriptures, and the strength we receive through the Sacraments, may we continue to imitate your faithful compassionate love for us, as individuals and as a couple.

Amen.

Ninth Sunday in Ordinary Time

Deuteronomy 5:12-15 2 Corinthians 4:6-11 Mark 2:23-3:6

'Earthenware jars'
Called to radiate God's Glory

For the Jewish people 'The Law', which included the Ten Commandments and the Book of the Covenant, contained many rituals governing worship. It also gave examples of both loving and unloving behaviour.

The Commandment to observe the Sabbath as a day of rest was given to the Israelites and also to us, as an opportunity for us to worship God. The Sabbath can also provide time for you, as couples, to reflect on how you, who are *'cracked and broken'* earthen-ware jars, formed by a loving God, can *'radiate' 'the face of God'* to the people with whom we celebrate the Eucharist every Sunday.

FOS

We are earthenware jars radiating God's glory.

PRAYER

Lord, thank you for the gift of the Sabbath, giving us time to 'renew, refresh and find joy' in our relationship with you and with each other.

We ask your guidance and help for couples who at this time have lost that joy in their relationship.

Amen.

Tenth Sunday in Ordinary Time

Genesis 3:9-15 ■ 2 Corinthians 4:13-5:1 ■ Mark 3:20-35

Together in Christ

Through the story of Adam and Eve in Genesis we learn what happened when they were disobedient and lost sight of God's plan for them. In his letter, Saint Paul advises that our troubles train us for eternal life, and Jesus, in the Gospel, reveals that all sins will be forgiven except the sin against the Holy Spirit.

We know how easy it is to blame each other (though notably it was Adam in the relationship who blamed Eve!). There are times in marriage when pressures and emotions are running so high that blaming is very tempting. We too can feel exposed and naked in our hurry to justify ourselves when things aren't right between us just like Adam and Eve when they were 'in trouble'.

This is the time to remind ourselves that the troubles we are experiencing or have experienced are *all* valuable on our journey together to eternal life. We realised a long time ago that marriage is a series of experiments in learning how to love one another. We would say sometimes, when we had failed or fallen short of our hopes and expectations, 'there goes another experiment'.

We must never lose sight of the fact that we are filled, and constantly refilled, with the Spirit. Grace is continuingly being poured upon us through our Sacrament of Marriage and the sacramental life of the Church. We have become *'a new creation in Christ'*. It is essential that we place our trust in one another but it is particularly important that we do this in the presence of God, who loves us unconditionally.

B&M

Together, strengthened by the Bread of Life.

PRAYER

Lord, we thank you and praise you for the constancy of your love.

May we continue to grow in acceptance of ourselves, each other, the power and blessings of your Holy Spirit, and our life in you.

Amen.

Eleventh Sunday in Ordinary Time

Ezekiel 17:22-24 ■ 2 Corinthians 5:6-10 ■ Mark 4:26-34

The seed that grows to become a shelter

"The Kingdom of God is like a mustard seed that grows into the largest shrub of all..."

Each of us has a seed of love in us at our birth, which is fostered as we grow to value others in our relationships. As we learn to love ourselves and each other more deeply the seed of love swells. As we learn about the qualities which give us and others freedom to be themselves, we can love ever more tenderly and discover God's peace and joy in our hearts. Seeds need sunshine and rain, periods of cold and warmth in order to grow, and so it is for us. In our marriage relationship we have a calling to continue deepening our love and intimacy. The ways in which we reach out to each other gently and tenderly, the experience of being listened to, the striving to listen and understand, the confidence which grows as we experience being understood, loved and accepted, as well as the forgiveness and healing we experience in times of hurt, are all ways in which the tree of our love can grow. It becomes a 'shelter' for our children, our families and all those whose lives we touch – a place where they find safety and acceptance.

What a wonderful and awe-inspiring invitation we have received to continually increase the depth of our love and yet at times it is difficult to do, but with God's help, we can achieve it.

M&L

Tender love shelters our family.

PRAYER

Lord, as we endeavour to grow closer together, we place ourselves in your hands.

Please be with us when we risk sharing our innermost thoughts, feelings and deep needs with each other.

Please give us the gifts of openness, acceptance and peace so that we can bring your Kingdom alive in our world.

Amen.

Twelfth Sunday in Ordinary Time

■ Job 38:1, 8-11 ■ 2 Corinthians 5:14-17 ■ Mark 4:35-41

When we pull together

There are, and have been, occasions in our marriage when we experienced stormy or turbulent times. These are times when events and situations seem larger than we can handle.

Events can overtake us and, as individuals, we can feel overwhelmed, almost at a loss about what to do about the situation we find ourselves in. The world out there sometimes seems to be against us no matter what we try to do. At such times no one seems to care and it can feel as if we are alone, tossed around from pillar to post!

When we don't share our anxieties and concerns with each other, the issues affecting us can appear to be much bigger than we can deal with as individuals. It's in situations like these that we need to remind ourselves of our love, care and concern for the other.

When we pull together we can face anything that the world may throw against us, safe in the knowledge of the real presence of the Lord who stills the storms of life with the words *"Quiet now! Be calm!"*

M&M

Together we can face what the world may throw against us.

PRAYER

Lord, help us to see that when we are weak we can call on your name for the courage to face whatever life may bring.

Strengthened in our love for each other and with hope and faith in you, may we be enabled to continue our journey together.

Amen.

Thirteenth Sunday in Ordinary Time

■ Wisdom 1:13-15; 2:23-24 ■ 2 Corinthians 8:7; 9:13-15
■ Mark 5:21-43

The triumph of love over fear

A striking sentence of this Sunday's Gospel reading is when Our Lord says to the official from the synagogue *'Do not be afraid. Only have faith'*. It reminds us of the times when we do not fully live up to our values because we are afraid and we lack the faith to believe that Our Lord will guide us and give us the strength to continue.

There are times when we are afraid of what people will think of us; of being bruised or feeling 'different', lonely and isolated from other people. As we struggle with these thoughts and feelings we can allow them to eat away so that they come between us. We can lose sight of the wonder of our husband or wife, and the beautiful person we know them to be, so we do not open our hearts to them.

The Gospel tells us to have faith, not to be afraid of living our values, to trust in Jesus' love and His presence with and in us. In sharing our pain with Him we can ask Him to give both of us courage and to bring the joy of our love alive again; we can find the openness to hear and accept the fear in the one who is afraid. We can also experience both the tenderness and gentleness that helps to draw us together and the deep peace that results. The experience of belonging to each other revitalises our love and helps us to gain the courage we need to be true to our values. In turn, this leads to a renewed sense of our own self-worth.

M&L

The triumph of love over fear.

PRAYER

Lord, the next time we are afraid, please help us to really believe that you love us as we are.

Help us always to be open to your healing love, to listening to each other, to hearing the hurts and pains of the past, the fear within each of us of being hurt again.

We ask you to fill us with your peace and joy that comes from your forgiving, healing love.

Amen.

Fourteenth Sunday in Ordinary Time

■ Ezekiel 2:2-5 ■ 2 Corinthians 12:7-10 ■ Mark 6:1-6

The beautiful qualities we bring to each other

A Prophet, in the Biblical sense, is not someone who predicts the future. It is someone who draws attention to the here and now, and this gives us the opportunity to reflect on the possible consequences of the situation we are in.

Saint Paul points out that when we are full of our own importance we can become arrogant and insensitive to the needs of others. At such times we can take others for granted, failing to see the amazing and beautiful qualities in those we think we know.

Jesus himself found it difficult to work miracles among his own family and friends! He was amazed at their lack of faith! They were unable to see Him for what He was.

For us in our marriage the challenge is to recognise the beautiful human qualities we bring to our life together and to give each other thanks and encouragement constantly for them. When we love in this way and when we make love we bring new life to each other and to our relationship. As Saint Paul points out, to do this requires us to leave behind our self-centredness and when we do this we become truly strong and our relationship is deeply enriched.

M&M

The beautiful qualities we bring to each other.

PRAYER

Lord, may we never fail to praise you for the fullness of life and salvation we bring to each other in our relationship and that you give us in this Eucharist.

Amen.

Fifteenth Sunday in Ordinary Time

Amos 7:12-15 Ephesians 1:3-14 Mark 6:7-13

Sent out in pairs

The concept of sending the apostles out in pairs to bring the Good News to the people is repeated in other parts of the New Testament. It is interesting to speculate that in some cases the people referred to were married couples.

The first twelve people to be sent out by Jesus (in six pairs) were made up of the first apostles; the Greek word for apostle means 'one sent out'. Later in the Gospel there are accounts of up to forty being sent out in pairs.

Jesus gave them detailed instructions for their mission. He no doubt chose to ensure the pairing off of those people He thought would work best together. It is possible that some of the pairs He sent out were married couples. If this is so it would be a rare recognition for those times of the special value that married couples have in the Church. A married couple can draw deep spiritual strength from their sacramental relationship and have much to offer others when they work together for the Church.

P&M

Sent out in pairs.

PRAYER

Lord, just as you sent out the apostles in pairs to preach the Good News, so let us learn to share responsibility for the mission you entrust to us.

Amen.

Sixteenth Sunday in Ordinary Time

Jeremiah 23:1-6 Ephesians 2:13-18 Mark 6:30-34

Walking alongside or away?

The Shepherd theme is evident in today's readings. In the first reading Jeremiah condemns the Jewish priests and kings, the shepherds of God's people, who allowed worship to go on in the pagan shrines throughout their kingdoms, and even in the Jerusalem Temple. Jeremiah promised that there would be a descendent of David who would bring true worship.

Jesus was that descendent of David. In spite of His teaching and the miracles He worked, Jesus, the Good Shepherd, experienced at times the pain of rejection. Many *'walked with him no longer'*. This can offer some consolation to you when despite your best efforts to pass on the Catholic faith to your children, you, their 'shepherds', can sometimes experience the pain of seeing them drifting away from the faith. At times you might even see them choosing lifestyles that are contrary to the Christian values you have sought to hand on to them. Your children, like all of us, need the constant guidance and strength of the Holy Spirit to counter the many evil influences at work in the world.

FOS

Some walked with him no longer.

PRAYER

Lord, thank you for the privilege of being entrusted by you with the responsibility of the physical, emotional, intellectual and spiritual well-being of our children, and for the joys and sorrows this has brought to our lives.

We are confident that you will always forgive our failures in our care of them.

Please touch their minds and hearts to enable them to live their lives in loving ways.

Amen.

Seventeenth Sunday in Ordinary Time

Kings 4:42-44 ■ Ephesians 4:1-6 ■ John 6:1-15

In selflessness, gentleness and patience

The glorious readings today are telling us of God's continuing faithfulness to his people, and their response. Elisha, who was accustomed to listening to God, tells the man in the first reading to feed one hundred people with the loaves and grain. "What?" the man asks, probably as we ourselves have asked when something that seems foolish or impossible is suggested to us. This is, of course, the forerunner to the Gospel story where Jesus feeds at least five thousand on a few loaves and fishes. These stories of God's providence, where on each occasion there is some left over, remind us of our faithful God who gives, and gives, and then gives some more. Saint Paul reminds the Ephesians that this God is the Father of all. He calls them to *'bear with one another charitably, in complete selflessness, gentleness and patience'* and to do all that they can *'to preserve the unity of the Spirit by the peace that binds you together.'* All that they can? All that *we* can? Sometimes it feels like enough is enough. I have given and given and given again to you, my beloved, and I have nothing more to give.

The question that arises here is this: in whose strength am I giving? Is it my own strength? When Jesus asks us to go the extra mile, we simply cannot do this if it is not in His strength. Sometimes what God is asking of us in our marriages might seem foolish and impossible, like the man being asked to feed one hundred people, but let us remember – God always gives us more than we need.

B&M

Bear with one another in gentleness and patience.

PRAYER

Lord, bountiful lover and provider, lead us to a deeper trust in your providence.

Help us to pray together more often and to listen attentively to that still small voice within, so that we may clearly discern your will for our marriage.

Amen.

Eighteenth Sunday in Ordinary Time

I Exodus 16:2-4, 12-15 · Ephesians 4:17, 20-24 · John 6:24-35

Courage and strength from the Bread of Life

In the readings for today, the focus is very much on God's love and care for each of us. If we trust in that love, He provides us with the Bread of Life, giving us the courage and strength to face up to and grow in each situation that occurs in our relationships, particularly with each other, for it is here that we can be most vulnerable.

When we have the faith to place ourselves in God's hands, the gifts that come to us through his grace are many. He blesses us with the gifts of patience, gentleness and kindness. He gives us the ability to listen, and understand, to forgive and to heal and many more gifts and graces.

Sometimes the demands of marriage on our energy, emotions and spiritual strength are so strong that it is very difficult to believe that Jesus is holding us in the palm of His hand. This has happened when one of us has suffered from mental or physical illness. There have been times when it has not seemed possible to communicate, when we rarely touched each other, and when we wanted to say things in our prayers that were difficult to say out loud to each other. At such times it was necessary for us to dig deep and find the trust that Jesus would pull us through and there would be a time in the future when we would be together again physically, emotionally and spiritually.

M&L

He provides us with courage and strength.

PRAYER

Lord, when the going gets very difficult please give us the deep faith that will enable us to trust that you are with us in our pain.

Please give us the courage to reach out to each other with tenderness and forgiveness in our hearts and help us to grow through these situations so that we can come together again and experience a renewed depth of our love.

Amen.

Nineteenth Sunday in Ordinary Time

I Kings 19:4-8 Ephesians 4:30 – 5:2 John 6:41-51

Enabled to love as God loves us

On our wedding day, through His sacramental blessing, the Father draws us to Himself. As Scripture points out *'The Holy Spirit of God has marked us with His seal in order to set us free.'* In this way we are enabled to love each other as He loves, wholly, completely, deeply.

When we promised *to love* each other on our wedding day, we became that very special and unique love-relationship; a married couple. When we strive to love each other as Jesus loves us, we become a fragrant offering to God. Together, strengthened by the Bread of Life, our married love is transformed into a sign of the presence of God, for everyone we come into contact with, here and now!

M&M

A married couple and God loves us.

PRAYER

Lord, bless and strengthen our love for each other in the everyday messiness of our lives.

We ask this so that our children and others might experience this same love which you give.

Amen.

Twentieth Sunday in Ordinary Time

■ Proverbs 9:1-6 ■ Ephesians 5:15-20 ■ John 6:51-58

Choose life

The passage from Ephesians is an exhortation to people to be careful about the lifestyle they live. It offers interesting parallels with changes that are often found in the lives of young married couples.

When the stag parties and the hen nights are over, after the last 'fling' as single people, and when the exhilaration of the wedding has passed it can seem that what is on offer lacks excitement. There may then be a temptation to return to 'old' ways, to a time when self-gratification seemed to offer the only way of life.

But Saint Paul urges us to be careful about the sort of lives we lead, wanting us to choose an intelligent lifestyle rather than living without good sense. The answer to the wickedness in the world around us is to let it be redeemed by the way we live our lives. This call to make choices about the way we live, rather than just drifting along with little thought, is an important choice that we don't always appreciate.

We do not have to follow those who would lead us into sinfulness. We can make a choice to be filled with the Holy Spirit and give thanks to the Lord for all he has given us.

P&M

Be careful to choose an intelligent lifestyle.

PRAYER

Lord, help us to remember that our Christian lives are constantly under observation by those who seek to destroy us.

We pray that you will protect and watch over us at all times.

Amen.

Twenty-First Sunday in Ordinary Time

Joshua 24:1-2, 15-18 ■ Ephesians 5:21-32 ■ John 6: 60-69

Making decisions: being open and honest

The readings today are about people making important choices. When Jesus told the crowd that they must eat His flesh and drink His blood or they would not have life in Him, many decided to stop being His followers. Jesus asked the Twelve if they also wanted to go away. Peter said: *"Lord, where shall we go to? You have the words of eternal life and we believe; we know that you are the Holy One of God"*. The second reading is about the most important decision that most people make, the decision to get married. It offers a beautiful vision of married love.

The mention of 'submit' in the passage from Ephesians raises many hackles in today's world of equality issues. 'Submit' does not mean obey. In fact the passage begins by saying that husbands and wives should submit themselves *to each other*. In this context 'submit' is about choosing to be open and honest with each other. Open, honest and trust-filled communication brings about intimacy.

Christ showed His love for His bride, the Church, by submitting Himself to the Father's will for the sake of the blessings His death would bring to us all. The passage pictures the Church as a virgin bride, prepared for her bridegroom by being cleansed completely by the action of the Word of God and the Holy Spirit. That is a reference to the holiness that comes about through husbands and wives living their lives in a way that is open to the word of God and the actions of the Holy Spirit.

FOS

Open honest trust-filled communication brings intimacy.

PRAYER

Lord, help us to be a 'sign' to our fellow Christians of the reality of your love.

Let the Church itself, through the choices we make in our lives together, become a sign to the world around us of this reality.

Amen.

Twenty-Second Sunday in Ordinary Time

■ Deuteronomy 4:1-2, 6-8 ■ James 1:17-18, 21-22, 27
■ Mark 7:1-8, 14-15, 21-23

Choosing what is best for 'us'

Interesting words are coming through in today's readings: 'note', 'observe', and although Moses does not quite say 'obey' he is telling the Israelites *"you must."* Saint James is saying *"accept and submit"* to the Word, *"you must"* do what the Word tells you rather than just listening to it and deceiving yourself. Ouch!

We read in the Gospel how Jesus almost affirms the fact that his disciples are breaking the rules. He talks of people only honouring him with lip-service while their hearts are far from him. In marriage, we can compare this to times when we behave in ways we consider to be 'husbandly' or 'wifely'. There can be times when we say the right words and do the right actions, yet our hearts can be far from genuine consideration of each other. It can be extremely difficult at times in a marriage to be a truly loving spouse. There can be two agendas which clash with each other, two different styles of parenting, and varying notions of how we use our money. We can also have different perceptions of how we celebrate our sexuality. The heart of the matter comes down to us choosing to do 'what the Word tells us.'

Jesus has promised that He is always with us; He said, *"where two or three gather in my name, I am there"*. What a gift we have as married couples; there are two of us! We can make listening to Jesus a lifestyle choice, enabling us to listen to each other more carefully. Listening to Jesus helps us to accept and submit to one another and this is what brings new life to our relationship.

B&M

A lifestyle choice – the two of us.

PRAYER

Lord, thank you for your abiding presence.

May we never take your presence for granted but always seek to allow you to be at the heart of our life together, our love, and the choices we make for the well-being of our marriage.

Amen.

Twenty-Third Sunday in Ordinary Time

Isaiah 35:4-7 James 2:1-5 Mark 7:31-37

Healing and wholeness may take time

One of the great joys of our married life together is the experience of healing. This is the healing that can take place when we come together after a time when one of us has felt hurt by the other. There may have been criticism, hurtful words or a painful silence between us. When the hurt is deep and it is hard to reach out to the other, it may take time for the negative feelings to subside to enable us to talk. When we have the faith to ask God for His courage, gentleness and sensitivity to reach out to each other, we are blessed with strength and vulnerability.

The healing may take some time. It might include time doing things together without necessarily talking about the problem, time doing things we enjoy. When we believe that we are blessed with the forgiveness of our Father, we will eventually be able to reach out to each other with forgiveness in our hearts. Then we experience the stage of deep reconciliation and a sealing kiss.

M&L

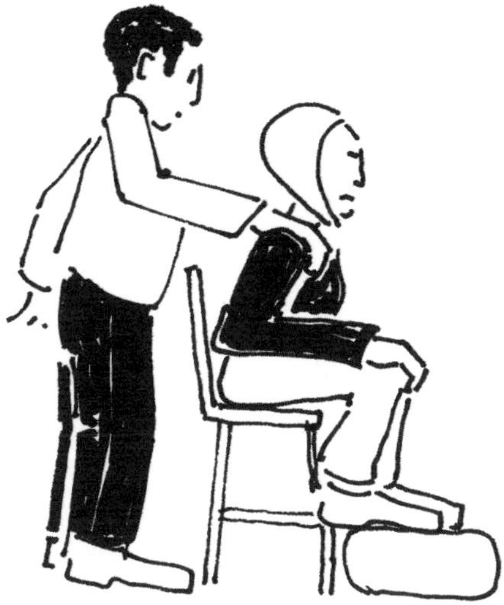

It may take time for the feelings to subside.

PRAYER

Lord, when we are the cause of hurt to each other, help us to remember that you are with us in our pain.

Help us to see our own faults and the beauty of our spouse; remove the bitterness we feel and help us to experience your healing love by the way we come together.

Amen.

Twenty-Fourth Sunday in Ordinary Time

Isaiah 50:5-9 James 2:14-18 Mark 8:27-35

Love in action: so that you know

Scripture teaches that words by themselves, even wonderful inspiring words, are not necessarily enough.

Jesus invites us, *"to love as He loves"*, and we hear this so often in the Scripture readings that there is a risk the words will become so familiar that we stop really hearing them. They become 'just words.'

We too, in our married relationships, can say the words *"I love you"* but without actions and intention the words may mean little or nothing. When we are speaking words of love we must act in a way that our partner knows we really love them.

It's easy to 'talk the talk' in marriage, but much harder to 'walk the walk'. It is through all my little acts of selfless giving that you know that I love you. It's through all the little things that you do for me that I know you love me!

In the way we give ourselves to each other, we grow to love each other more. Through our self-sacrifice we gain the love of the other.

M&M

So that you know, I love you.

PRAYER

Lord, I place all my trust in you.

Help me in my weakness to see and experience you through the tender, powerful love of my husband / my wife.

Amen.

Twenty-Fifth Sunday in Ordinary Time

Wisdom 2:12, 17-20 James 3:16-4:3 Mark 9:30-37

Selfish ambition versus intimacy

The readings for today are full of the struggle between goodness exemplified by the peacemakers, and the wickedness of those driven by jealousy and selfish ambition.

The Apostle James recognises that this conflict really stems from individuals seeking to draw others into their wickedness.

The Godless urge others to join them in acts of cruelty against those who are seen as virtuous, testing if God will rescue the gentle from their clutches. Saint James also points out that wars and battles between us usually stem from the desire to have things or achieve selfish ambitions that are not in our best interests.

Married couples tend to act together, and to regulate what they do as a couple. They know each other much more intimately than they are known to other people and this gives them a double check on their actions. Their consciences are reinforced by the extent to which they are prepared to be open and honest with their partner. To put it bluntly, in marriage it is difficult to get away with many actions that a single person could conceal from others.

P&M

Because they know each other intimately they have a double check.

PRAYER

Lord, help us to remain open to those who have our good welfare at heart, and to learn to discern that which is beneficial from that which is harmful to us.

Amen.

Twenty-Sixth Sunday in Ordinary Time

Numbers 11:25-29 · James 5:1-6 · Mark 9:38-43, 45, 47-48

Attitudes stemming from jealousy

In today's readings, Moses and Jesus were faced by critics who complained about their attitude to people who were doing things that some in their society thought they were not authorized to do. Both Moses and Jesus ignored the criticism, recognising that jealousy was behind the negative attitudes.

How many evils have been perpetrated against individuals or groups as a result of jealousy? The media focuses too much attention on celebrities, on people's status, possessions, income, physical appearance and sexual performance. It is easy to develop a habit of using these criteria when measuring one's own or other people's worth, and in some cases, become jealous of those who look better, have more money or possessions, or a higher status. When we fall into this trap we see ourselves as lacking in certain aspects. This can lead us to resent what we see others have and judge them unfairly.

This resentment can become so strong that it can lead to words or actions intended to harm the other person or group, or damage their good name. It can affect relationships when husbands and wives are tempted to judge their spouse on their ability to match up to what the media shows us. Recent research has concluded that as many as one in six marriages end because of attitudes or behaviour stemming from jealousy. Jealousy could be seen as a silly sin, because it principally harms the person who is jealous, but it is a sad fact that jealousy can become so deep-seated that it can cause serious harm to others.

FOS

PRAYER

Lord, help us to respect and value the worth of each person as someone created and loved by you.

May we never allow the false values, so often exalted by the media in all its forms, to lead us to adopt attitudes or behaviour that stem from jealousy of other people's possession, money, status or attainments.

Amen.

Twenty-Seventh Sunday in Ordinary Time

Genesis 2:18-24 Hebrews 2:9-11 Mark 10:2-16

Two in one flesh

It was the Lord God who said, *"It is not good that the man should be alone. I will make him a helpmate."* According to this version in the book of Genesis, the Lord God built the woman from the rib of the man, *"Bone from my bones and flesh from my flesh,"* says the man. He was incomplete until his partner was created. Man and woman are made to be two in one flesh, mates and helpmates for life.

There must have been failure in Biblical times to live up to that high ideal because, in the Gospel, we have the Pharisees seeking to test Jesus. Moses, they said, allowed divorce, so what did Jesus have to say about that? *"It was because you were so unteachable that he wrote this commandment for you,"* Jesus replied.

When we look at the world around us it would be easy to draw the conclusion that we are still unteachable. Nobody wants to see a couple locked into a loveless marriage and many of us will be aware of the damage done to the children where the parents have stayed in a marriage that has broken down. In today's world, how does the Bible's teaching apply to our own marriages? Have I asked myself recently who is this person that I live with, that I call husband or wife? Do I really know you, my beloved? When was the last time that we celebrated our sexuality, the pinnacle of our being two in one flesh? How much of a priority is our lovemaking in our life currently? How much of a priority are you?

B&M

We celebrate our sexuality. Two in one.

PRAYER

Lord, continue to grace our marriage with the gift of us praising, affirming and celebrating each others goodness.

May our relationship be a source of life to us and all those we love and care for.

Amen.

Twenty-Eighth Sunday in Ordinary Time

Wisdom 7:7-11 Hebrews 4:12-13 Mark 10:17-30

The call to change: hers or mine or ours?

On our wedding day, we made the commitment to love each other for the rest of our lives; growing in love together so that everyone who came to know us would see a sign of Jesus' love for all mankind.

Although we did not use those words on our wedding day, we promised essentially to change the things that come between us and to develop the things that bring us together. The Gospel calls us to share all that we have. This includes our gifts and talents as well as our material wealth, so in marriage there should never be an attitude of 'mine' or 'his' and 'hers'.

Yet we know from experience that we cannot cope with too much change that comes too fast. Wisdom tells us that it is the journey we are making towards each other that is important, rather than how far we have come or how far we have to go. When we try and change too much too fast, we feel resentment and our journey together can come to a temporary stop. It is important that we keep in touch with ourselves and our own development and ensure that every change we make, we make willingly.

M&L

Not mine or hers or his.

PRAYER

Lord, please give us the zeal to want to change for each other, the insight to see what changes will bring us closer together and the wisdom to know what changes I can make now.

Amen.

Twenty-Ninth Sunday in Ordinary Time

Isaiah 53:10-11 Hebrews 4:4-16 Mark 10:35-45

Approaching the other, approaching the throne of grace

The Scripture today speaks about not lauding it over one another, reminding us that on our wedding day we each became a 'gift' to the other. Spelling that out, it means we come to one another with an attitude of total giving, without reservation of any kind, without expectation, but with great hope in each others love.

We are invited to have complete confidence in our beloved; able to approach each other with desire, knowing that in our vulnerability we will be received with tenderness and love!

It is to this kind of love that we aspire knowing that, at our weakest, we are at our strongest in our married love.

In aspiring to love each other in this way we can experience the height and depth of which human love is capable when blessed by God.

M&M

Always able to approach each other.

PRAYER

Lord, may the gift of our lives to each other bring us your love and forgiveness.

May we serve you through our love for each other.

Amen.

Thirtieth Sunday in Ordinary Time

Jeremiah 31:7-9 · Hebrews 5:1-6 · Mark 10:46-52

Ministering to and with one another

In his Letter to the Hebrews, Saint Paul gives us an in depth perspective on the priesthood when he speaks of the limitations of weakness. Saint Paul refers to the need for priests to make sin offerings for themselves as well as for the people.

Those who serve as ministers working in the Church can sometimes be tempted to inflate their importance. It is important to remember that no one takes the honour of ministry on himself or herself because each one is individually called by God.

It is not usual in the Church for married couples to be given the gift of ministry as *a couple*. When this has been tried, it is often found that particular graces flow, especially those graces related to relationship. It is also possible for husbands and wives to act as moderating influences for each other if one of them loses clear sight of the mission that God has called them to.

P&M

The gift of ministry as a couple.

PRAYER

Lord, help us always to be aware of the need for humility, as we seek to fulfil the mission you entrust to us.

Amen.

Thirty-First Sunday in Ordinary Time

Deuteronomy 6:2-6 ■ Hebrews 7:23-28 ■ Mark 12:28-34

Offering ourselves: in sickness and in health

Before the time of Jesus' death, the standard for loving was that given by the Scribe: *'You must love the Lord your God with all your heart, with all your soul, with all your mind and with all your strength. The second commandment is this: You must love your neighbour as yourself'*.

The second reading includes this phrase: *'...because he has done this once for all by offering himself'*. That act of offering Himself was the greatest act of love God has ever shown the human race, and at the same time, it was the greatest act of love any human being has ever shown to God.

That act of unconditional love provided a new standard against which to measure our loving. Jesus loved the Father with all his heart, soul, mind and strength. So should we. But in loving others, He provided us with a new standard by which to judge our words and actions: *'love one another with the same unconditional love with which I have loved you'*. That was the kind of love you promised to show when you took each other, *'for better for worse, for richer for poorer, in sickness and in health, to love and to cherish, till death do us part'.*

FOS

In sickness and in health.

PRAYER

Lord, thank you for the love you have placed in our hearts, and for all it has brought to our lives.

Whatever the difficulties we are called to face, give us the help and strength we need to continue living out each day the commitment to you and to each other that we made on our wedding day.

Amen.

Thirty-Second Sunday in Ordinary Time

■ Kings 17:10-16 ■ Hebrews 9:24-28 ■ Mark 12:38-44

Giving from the little that we have

The common thread running through this Sunday's readings seems to be about sacrifice, though widows are fairly prominent too. In the First Book of Kings, we hear how the widow's response to her godly visitor was blessed with an abundance of food left over, though shortly before she and her son had been about to die of starvation. Mark's Gospel features Jesus telling us of the bountiful gift of the widow, when she gave what little she had. Saint Mark compares it to those who seemingly gave a lot, yet it was only a small proportion of their possessions. The Letter to the Hebrews reminds us that Jesus gave everything of himself, once and for all, and that He will come again with the promised salvation for all of us who anticipate that day.

The Latin root for the two syllables making the word sacrifice are holy (sacri...) and making (...fice) There can be a very negative way of looking at 'sacrificing' within marriage, seeing it as giving in, or giving up something of ourselves that is important or really necessary for us.

When we look at the context of these readings, it is easier to see clearly the 'holiness' inherent in the 'sacrifices' of all those involved. On reflection, the reality of our life's experiences tells us that it is through giving that we receive so much. The small things that we do for one another each day produce wonderful and fruitful consequences in our marriage. It is our daily 'yes' to each other that is ultimately 'making us holy'.

B&M

PRAYER

Lord, thank you so much for all the times you have graced us to say 'yes' and 'I will' and 'I do', and for all the love that has flowed from our sacrifices.

Be with us today as we continue to strive to give of our best to each other and to you.

Amen.

Thirty-Third Sunday in Ordinary Time

Daniel 12:1 – 3 Hebrews 10:11 – 14; 18 Mark 13:24 – 32

We do not know the hour or the day

Today, the Scripture readings remind us that our world will not go on forever. This in turn reminds us that our relationship will not last forever. For most of us, the death of either of us seems a long way into the future and it is not something that we think of or talk about.

Yet, on a few occasions, we have tried to imagine life without the other. We have considered the emptiness of such a life; with no one to roll over and cuddle first thing in the morning; no one to bring tea to; no one with whom to share morning prayer; all these are examples of the absence of the little things that made life together so special. When we consider the intense black loneliness of not being together, it's then that we begin to touch the depth of what we mean to each other.

M&L

After you… oh!

PRAYER

Lord, thank you for our life together, for each moment that we share.

We know that you are with us in our love.

Please help us to treasure each moment we have together, never to take each other for granted and never to miss an opportunity to let each other know the depth of our love.

Amen.

Last Sunday of the Year
The Feast of Christ the King

■ I Daniel 7:13-14 ■ Revelation 1:5-8 ■ John 18:33-37

Called to bring joy

On this last Sunday of the Church's year we celebrate Christ the King. Jesus is the King of the Universe and His Kingdom is for everyone. We are asked, in our humanity, to live in the imitation of Christ the King.

We are reminded that we too, in our married love, are to be a '*kingdom of love*' where truth, life, holiness, grace, justice, desire, passion, tenderness, peace, and 'the oil of gladness' are all experienced.

When we choose to live in this way, our love for each other will bring life, joy, and peace to everyone we know. This may seem impossible but it is not a tall order for God! With Him on our side who can be against us?

M&M

Bring joy to everyone we know.

PRAYER

Lord, we praise and thank you for the many gifts and blessings we have received throughout our married life.

We ask that we continue to be graced and blessed so we may always be a sign of your love for our children, our family and our church.

Amen.

The Immaculate Conception of The Blessed Virgin Mary

Genesis 3:9-15, 20 ■ Ephesians 1:3-6, 11-12 ■ Luke 1:26-38

God's invitation calls for our co-operation

The disobedience of our first parents described in the first reading was something foreseen by the Blessed Trinity before human beings were created. This is made clear in the second reading where Saint. Paul mentions that God, '*before the world was made,*' had a plan, centred in Christ, that included his choice of us '*to be holy and spotless and to live through love in his presence*', chosen to be '*his adopted sons, through Jesus Christ*', chosen to be for His greater glory '*the people who would put their hopes in Christ before he came*'.

If that choice included us, it must surely have included the choice of Mary, 'the one '*so highly favoured*' by God. But the choice of Mary by God did not mean she lacked the freedom to choose. Mary was given grace in a special way because of God's choice of her to be the mother of His Son. From the moment of her conception in the womb of her mother, Anne, she was kept free of the 'macula' or stain of sin by God's special help. Mary was tempted, just like her son Jesus, and like our first parents but she used the graces given her by God to help her overcome temptation. Mary remained free from sin throughout her life.

She had said '*Yes*' to God freely, and she saw this as enabling God's plan for our '*salvation through Christ*' to be fulfilled. If you, like Mary, accept God's choice to be husband, wife, often parents, you have good reason to believe that the fulfilment of the purpose of His call depends on your co-operation with His grace at every moment of your lives.

FOS

The fulfilment of His call depends on our co-operation with His grace.

PRAYER

Lord, you have called us by our Baptism and by our Marriage Covenant with you to play our part in your saving plan for the human race.

In thanking you for your call, we ask you to give us the graces we need to play our part in the working out of your saving plan, through the choices we make.

Amen.

The Presentation of the Lord

Malachi 3:1-4 Hebrews 2:14-18 Luke 2:22-40

Lord, the light of your love is shining

According to the Law of Moses every first born male child must be consecrated to the Lord. Essentially this involved a purification procedure for Mary and Joseph and a dedication of the child Jesus. To authenticate this consecration, a sacrifice must be made, and since Mary and Joseph were poor they could only afford the simplest offering – two turtle doves or a pair of young pigeons. One might imagine the couple waiting at the entrance to the temple, wondering if they have got their instructions right. Joseph was perhaps a little ashamed that their sacrifice was so basic and Mary reassuring him his offering was fully in accordance with the law. As they hesitate at the entrance a strange man comes by, seizes the child in his arms and begins praising God. Joseph might well have feared for the child's safety but again Mary could have reassured him for now she was beginning to realise that something out of the ordinary was taking place. Simeon, for that is the old man's name, is saying something about Jesus being the '*salvation for all to see*'. He is also saying that Jesus is to be a sign – but a sign that would be rejected. They did not understand what all this meant, and how often we too fail to understand our calling in the plan of salvation.

So, when all had been done according to the law, Mary and Joseph and Jesus left Jerusalem and began the journey back to Nazareth. We might imagine the couple making their way, singing God's praises for the beautiful child He had given them, dimly aware that they carried in their arms the Salvation of the entire world. We too can be unaware so often of our role in helping one another along the road to salvation.

P&M

May the light that is revealed, transform us.

PRAYER

Lord, may the light that is revealed by the words of Simeon at the Presentation of Jesus, enter our hearts and bring us true salvation.

Amen.

Saint Joseph

I Samuel 7:4-5, 12-14, 16 Romans 4:13, 16-18, 22
Matthew 1:16, 18-21, 24

A model husband

In todays first reading God tells David that his throne will last forever. In the Gospel we see the fulfilment of this promise when 'Joseph, son of David,' takes Mary to his home and subsequently Jesus is born in David's Royal City, Bethlehem.

The Bible tells us very little about Joseph, but we can assume he must have been a very reliable person since God chose him to be the spouse of Mary, and entrusted both her and Jesus to his care.

Although Joseph was at first overwhelmed by the responsibility God had placed in him, after he received a message in a dream he accepted his responsibilities for Mary and the baby and trusted that God would give him all the physical, emotional and spiritual help he would need. We can only imagine the concerns he must have had when the family had to emigrate to Egypt, and some years later when twelve year old Jesus stayed behind in the Temple and his parents thought he was lost. Traditionally, Joseph has been given to us as Protector of the Church – because he and Mary were its first members: Patron of Workers – because he was a carpenter; Patron of the Dying – because Mary and Jesus were with him when he died.

Mary and Joseph are a model for married couples in their love for God and for each other. Joseph is also a model for husbands in the way they should care for their wives and children, and an example for fathers to follow, because of the way he must have prayed for God's help as he cared for Mary and Jesus.

FOS

Saint Joseph is a model for husbands in their care for their wives and children.

PRAYER

Lord, thank you for the joy you have given us in our relationship as a couple. Thank you too, for our children.

May we continue to receive the help we need in our care for each other, our children, and others through the prayers of Joseph.

Amen.

The Annunciation of the Lord

Isaiah 7:10-14 Hebrews 10:4-10 Luke 1:26-38

God invites and we co-operate, Christ is born anew

The letter to the Hebrews reflects on the changes that took place as Jesus illustrated (throughout His life) that holiness comes not from obedience to rules, but to the will of God. We ourselves affirm this in the responsorial psalm.

Mary must have been steeped in the Scriptures to have been able to respond to God's messenger as she did. She hears an invitation from an angel that cannot possibly make any sense to her, a virgin, and she asks how this could happen. On hearing the angel's reply, she says, "*Be it done to me according to your will.*" In her simplicity of heart, Mary's wish was to do God's will. The angel's invitation was followed by Mary's co-operation, which lead to the Incarnation of Jesus: God among us.

God's plan for Mary and for Joseph is quite different from his plan for any of us but the same elements are there. We are *invited* to do the will of God, we can choose to *co-operate*, and in each act of love we offer to each other, each 'yes' we say to our husband, our wife, Christ is born in us anew and this is *Incarnation*.

The Letter to the Hebrews says that '*His will was for us to be made holy by the offering of His body*'. As Christian couples we are called to live Christ's message in our world. Each time we offer our bodies, whether in the kitchen or the bedroom, the workplace or the garden, we are obeying God's will and bringing His light and life into our world.

B&M

Each yes we say,
Christ is born again.

PRAYER

Lord, may we too learn to be steeped in your ways, so that we might hear your invitation ever more clearly.

Please help us to co-operate with your grace, and obey your will as we seek to follow your example with loving tenderness in our own marriage.

Amen.

Holy Trinity

Deuteronomy 4:32-34, 39-40 Romans 8:14-17
Matthew 28:16-20

The Blessed Trinity is an intimate love relationship

Moses said to the people, "*Understand this today, and take it to heart: The Lord is God indeed, in heaven above as on earth beneath, he and no other.*" Moses told the Jewish people to keep God's laws and commandments.

In Saint Paul's letter to the Romans, Paul is telling the people that they are God's children, heirs of God, and co-heirs with Christ, because they have been moved by and received the Spirit of God. This applies equally to all of us. In the Gospel we hear Jesus telling His disciples to go out to all the nations, baptising them in the name of the Father, the Son and the Holy Spirit. We hear Him telling the disciples to "*know that I am with you always; yes, to the end of time.*" This is what He wants us to know too. There is a lot of 'telling the people' in this Sunday's readings.

Over the cacophony of sound that fills our lives, what can we hear today? Jesus assured His disciples that the commandments can be summed up in love of God and love of neighbour. The intimacy of married love has this high calling. We are called to love each other because we are each other's closest neighbour, and we are also called to love God and this is something we can share in together. It has been said that married love can most closely reveal the love relationships in the Trinity. Where we recognise three persons in One God, we can see the call and the challenge to us as married couples to become two persons in one flesh.

B&M

The intimacy of married love that has the highest calling.

PRAYER

Lord, we ask for the grace to deepen our appreciation of the divine life we share in within your love as Father, Son and Holy Spirit.

May we come to know your presence, guidance and inspiration and allow these gifts to motivate and move us to let the power of our love shine out in your world.

Amen.

Corpus Christi
(The Body and Blood of Christ)

Exodus 24:3-8 Hebrews 9:11-15 Mark 14:12-16, 22-26

Me becomes 'we', two in one

The covenant of blood that Moses made with God on behalf of all the people is now replaced with the covenant of blood that Jesus Christ made with the Father when he offered himself as atonement for our sins. Jesus made it clear to the Apostles what he was going to offer and how the memorial of his sacrifice was to be enacted for all time. Jesus said "*Whoever eats my flesh and drinks my blood will live in me and I in him.*" This was not easy for the Apostles to understand and it's not something that we today can comprehend easily either. The idea that bread could become the Body of Christ, living bread to be consumed by us is hard to take on board.

We can find some help in grasping this great mystery present in the sacrament of Matrimony. Two people, a man and a woman, freely choose to unite their lives, to be as one. This goes even further; they are called to be formed into a Trinitarian relationship of man, woman and God. This is something that can be witnessed. A man and a woman, two independent people, choose to forgo their individual selves and become a new thing, a 'couple', to let go of 'me' and become 'we' – two into one flesh.

When a couple embraces a sacramental relationship, other people can see the transformation. They see that showing care and concern for each other's welfare becomes more important than self-concern. What can also be visible is the way that sharing love in their daily lives is something that fulfils them. In this way the couple call their brothers and sisters in Christ to a depth of relationship that could otherwise have seemed impossible. In living in this way we are sustained by the Body and Blood of our Lord Jesus Christ.

P&M

Me becomes 'we', two in one flesh.

PRAYER

Lord, you nourish us with your Body and Blood given to us under the form of bread and wine.

We pray that the blessings we receive through our matrimonial spirituality enable us to help bring your love into the world.

Amen.

The Sacred Heart of Jesus

Hosea 11:1, 3-4, 8-9 Ephesians 3:8-12, 14-19 John 19:31-37

Tender, loving, forgiveness, even when we walk away

A loving father leading a child as it begins to walk '*with strings of love...*' Hosea provides us with a beautiful reminder of the reality of the tender love of God for the Jewish people. But, like so many parents, God had to watch his children go off to 'do their own thing' and suffer the consequences. Yet despite the sadness and the anger he could not abandon them '*because I am God not man*'.

Many parents, having discovered with Saint Paul '*the infinite treasure of Christ*' must also have prayed with Saint Paul that the Holy Spirit would enable the 'hidden self' in each of their children to grow strong, so they would come '*to grasp the breadth and the length, the height and the depth of the love of Christ, and be filled with the utter fullness of God*'. What God desires for all of us is that our 'hidden self' grows strong through a loving, life-giving relationship with Him.

The supreme evidence of that desire can be seen in the death of Jesus on the Cross; when His Sacred Heart was pierced by the centurion's lance, out flowed blood and water. This is symbolic of the tender loving forgiveness of God that pours into our minds, hearts and spirits through the Sacraments. This is echoed in the response to today's Psalm, that '*with joy you will draw water from the wells of salvation*'.

FOS

A child begins to walk with strings of love.

PRAYER

Lord, like our forefathers in the faith, we thank you for your tender compassionate love that continually forgives us, and draws us back to each other and to you.

As we reveal our 'hidden selves' to each other, through the grace of the Holy Spirit, may that same Spirit also strengthen our growth by the help we receive through the Sacraments.

Amen.

The Birth of John the Baptist

Isaiah 49:1-6 ■ Acts 13:22-26 ■ Luke 1:57-66, 80

Called by God in a unique sacrament

In today's readings there is a great sense that John the Baptist was someone special in God's eyes. Right from his birth, it was clear that he had been chosen for a special task. It is much harder to believe that God has selected the two of us to live in a unique Sacrament of Marriage and that our lives together will play a special part in God's mission if we allow Him to guide us.

Most of us find it easier to identify with the words in Isaiah "*I have toiled in vain. I have exhausted myself for nothing*" than to hear God saying, "*You are my servant in whom I shall be glorified.*" And yet we are told that it is through the openness and honesty that we have with each other that we are drawn closer to God. It is through our intimacy with each other that we find joy in our relationship and this also helps others to begin to understand the depth of God's love for us.

M&L

God has selected us to live in a unique sacrament.

PRAYER

Lord, help us to hear when you say "You are my servant in whom I shall be glorified."

Help us to see that our love is an important part of your plan for the world.

Give us the trust to be open and honest with each other with a deep gentleness and sensitivity so that we may experience the joy of Zechariah and the people round him.

Help us not to be blinded and disillusioned by the times that we have failed but believe in your call to intimacy and your willingness to forgive us.

Help us to forgive each other.

Amen.

Feast of Saints Peter and Paul

Acts of the Apostles 3:1-10 · Galatians 1:11-20 · John 21:15-19

Called by God to proclaim unity

Just as Peter and Paul were called in a special way to proclaim the Good News of Jesus to the world, we too have been called, through our marriage, to be signs to our Church of the love of God for His people.

We are no longer just 'him and her' but we are now 'Husband and Wife' with the mission to proclaim 'Unity' to our children, our family and the Church.

Just as Peter was freed by the Angel to proclaim God's saving power, we too, as man and woman have been freed by God's grace to love openly and honestly, nourishing each other with words and gestures of desire and tenderness.

We are called to become a unique and special sign to God's people of His saving grace and presence in the modern world, through our love for each other, for our children, our family and friends.

M&M

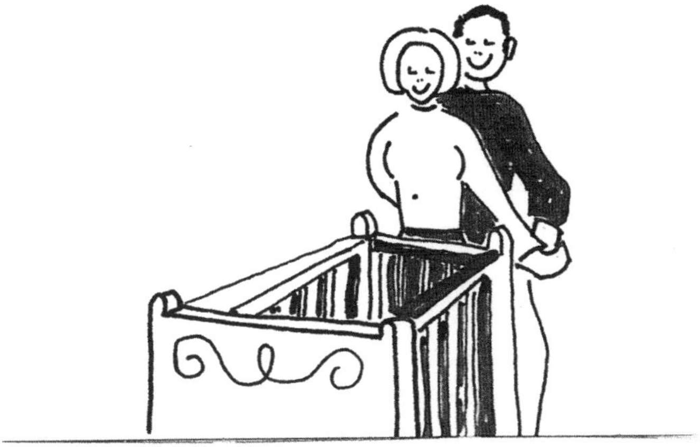

We are husband and wife
proclaiming unity to our family and church.

PRAYER

Lord, free us from all occasions of selfish thought and behaviour, so that together we may become, more and more, a powerful and holy sign of your love for your Church and our world.

Amen.

The Transfiguration of the Lord

■ Daniel 7:9-10, 13-14 ■ 2 Peter 1:16-19 ■ Mark 9:2-10

A fraction of that holy light

"Jesus took with him Peter and James and his brother John and led them up a high mountain where they could be alone. There in their presence he was transfigured; his face shone like the sun and his clothes became white as the light".

Perhaps the closest we can come to an awareness of the transfigured Christ occurs during the celebration of a Christian wedding. At a certain moment the couple become intensely aware of each other – often this occurs when they exchange vows, when they look deeply into each other's eyes with a look of love and tenderness. It is as though for them no-one else is present, as if a brilliant spotlight shines only on them. At this moment it could be said that they are transfigured for each other. There can be a communication of love so intense that it cannot be sustained for long and the couple "return" to the ceremony.

Of course it cannot be claimed that a loving moment for a couple, however special, is comparable to Jesus revealing his glory to the disciples. However, in human terms it helps us to begin to appreciate the wonder of the radiant glory that Jesus revealed. Such revelation is only to be seen briefly. The apostles were permitted only a glimpse of what lay ahead.

We too should watch out for the times when we are granted a brief look at God's power and majesty and love. These are stepping stones on our journey, and to miss them is to lose a precious gift.

P&M

A fraction of that holy light.

PRAYER

Lord, you revealed yourself to Peter, James and John, when you were transfigured.

May a tiny fraction of that holy light fall upon us so that we too may be transformed in your service.

Amen.

The Assumption of the Blessed Virgin Mary

Revelation 11:19, 12:1-6, 10 ■ 1 Corinthians 15:20-26
■ Luke 1:39-56

Our joys, trials and sufferings

On this Feast of the Assumption we celebrate the belief that because Mary was conceived without sin in the womb of her mother Anne, she did not suffer the penalty for sin, the corruption of her body, but was taken up body and soul into heaven immediately after her death.

In the second reading, Paul says the resurrection of Jesus is '*the first-fruits of those who have fallen asleep, and then, all who belong to him*' will be resurrected. Mary was the first of these. The first reading presents Mary in heaven as the woman who brought forth a male child (Jesus) and is now crowned with twelve stars (symbols of the twelve Apostles) in heaven, '*where God had made a place for her*'.

In the Gospel account of her great hymn, the Magnificat, Mary prophesies that '*all generations will call me blessed, for the almighty has done great things for me*'.

We have good reasons for believing that from her special place in heaven God continues to do great things through Mary. Her own experience of life on earth has made Mary very aware of the joys, trials and sufferings of life for married couples. This means you can turn to her with confidence whenever you are in need of her help.

FOS

The joys, trials and the sufferings of married couples.

PRAYER

Mary, our Mother, we thank you for all the blessings we have received in the past through the help of your prayers.

We know that your prayers are powerful with your Son, so we turn to you with confidence asking your prayers for... (mention any special need).

Amen.

The Triumph (or Exultation) of the Cross

■ Numbers 21:4-9 ■ Philippians 2:6-11 ■ John 3:13-17

Love can overcome everything: it is a decision

The words 'TRIUMPH' and 'CROSS' seem uncomfortable bedfellows lying uneasily together, but as in much of life, and faith, truth can often be found in paradox. Many sentiments from today's readings resonate with the 'truth' of life that is lived out in relationship. In the first reading we hear of people losing patience and questioning why they are in the mess they find themselves in. The second reading talks about becoming subservient, of humbling oneself, of dying a 'death' to selfishness which ultimately leads to new life, new hope and a new beginning. The Gospel reading shows that love can overcome everything when we believe in that love. These are all recurring realities of the challenges and joys of married life.

We can sometimes lose patience with the ones we love and question the quality of our relationship. We can ask ourselves why our spouse sometimes says the things they do, and this can lead us to think "Is this the best I can hope for? Isn't it about time he or she learned to do this, that, or the other?" There are times when, for the sake of love, we deny our own preferences, keeping our thoughts and opinions to ourselves and this can lead to us 'suffering' the sense of losing our own identity. Yet it is through such experiences, when we make the decision to believe in the other person and the love we share, that we discover the new life that Jesus promised.

This is the paradox, in the ebb and flow of relationship. Such are the graces to be found in and through the Sacrament of Marriage. When we paraphrase the Gospel ending we see that as husband and wife we were 'sent' to one another, not to condemn each other, but that, through our Sacrament of Marriage, we might be saved and so might those we love.

B&M

The decision to love.

PRAYER

Lord, we pray that we may deepen our belief in one another and may more readily recognise each others goodness and beauty.

Help us to affirm and encourage each other more often so that in, through and with our love you may be honoured and glorified.

Amen.

The Forty Martyrs of England and Wales

Hebrews 11:33-40 John 12:24-26

In our weakness we are strong

What we would like people to say of us is that 'these were people that through faith conquered kingdoms, did what is right and earned the promises. They were weak people who were given strength.'

It is so easy to see only the times when we were weak, the times when we did not listen, the times when we pressed on with an idea of our own independently of our spouse, or the times when we nursed our own hurts instead of trying to forgive.

We also need to recognise the times when we do reach out to each other and it is important to believe that, through prayer, we will be given the strength we need to be true to the promise '*to have and to hold*'.

M&L

They were weak people who were given strength.

PRAYER

Lord, as we wonder at the faithfulness of these men and women, help us to remember that the faithfulness of our love for each other is so important to you.

When we seem to be emotionally far apart from each other, please give us the grace to listen and to forgive, and help our relationship to grow through your forgiveness and love.

Amen.

All Saints

Revelation 7:2-4, 9-14 ■ I John 3:1-3 ■ Matthew 5:1-12

Nothing is missed by God

Our faithfulness and love for each other will unite us with all the Saints. On this Feast of all the Saints we are reminded that all the acts of kindness, tenderness, help and care that we give to each other and to others, no matter how large or how small, are being sanctified and made holy. Nothing, no matter how small, and no one, no matter how little they think of themselves, is missed or forgotten by God.

As the opening prayer of the Mass reminds us ... '*today we rejoice in the holy men and women of every time and place*'. In the first reading we hear:

'*After that I saw a huge number, impossible to count, of people from every nation, race, tribe, and language; they were standing in front of the throne and in front of the Lamb, dressed in white robes and holding palms in their hands*'.

We too are amongst that throng, dressed in our wedding garments. As we try to live out the Beatitudes with and for each other, the last words of the Gospel spell out the call to unity we have tried to live and to which we responded on our wedding day.

"Happy are you when people abuse you and persecute you and speak all kinds of calumny against you on my account. Rejoice and be glad for your reward will be great in heaven."

M&M

Nothing no matter how small...

PRAYER

Lord, help us to be poor in spirit, to be empty except for the love we have for each other, our Church and for you.

Amen.

All Souls

Isaiah 25:6-9 Romans 5:5-11 John 6:37-40

The more we share the less we regret

We celebrate All Souls day by remembering those of our families and communities who have died over the last year and beyond. This remembrance can be a time of sorrowing, tears and grief, yet the readings for today speak of celebration and rejoicing. For many people the death that is dreaded above all is that of a spouse. The loss of parents, children and close friends can be a time of great sorrow, but the death of a husband or wife can be so devastating that it seems that nothing can be said or done to 'reach' the bereaved spouse. The first time a widow or widower returns alone to their marital home, the place that holds so many memories of their life together, can seem like the loneliest moment of their life.

It may be, as Isaiah tells us, that '*the Lord will prepare a banquet for all; that he will remove the mourning veil covering all people; that he will wipe away the tears from every cheek*'. It may be; but it is very hard for a bereaved spouse to even begin to grieve, or to contemplate life without their loving companion, to recall things that were left unsaid or not done and now can never be shared. However, something can be done or said before death strikes. A wise old priest explained that if a married couple learn to share their feelings really fully during life, then the sense of loss and regret for things not shared is diminished.

The feelings of remorse cannot be eliminated, but if there are very few issues that have not been shared and if the heart is filled with a sense of togetherness then there is less room for regret. The closeness that comes from learning to share in a couple's life-time is also a preparation for coping with the separation that death brings. It also means that, paradoxically, at the right time, they will be able to offer support to other people who have been bereaved.

P&M

The more we share the less we regret.

PRAYER

Lord, help us to fill our lives with care and concern for our spouse, so that we can face death without fear or regret.

Amen.

Contributors

Brian & Maureen Devine
maurbri13@yahoo.co.uk

Mark & Liz Dutton
lizmark@lizmarkl.co.uk

Maurice & Margaret Magee
mwmmmagee@me.com

Canon Frank O' Sullivan
frnksul@tiscali.co.uk

Peter & Maureen Watson
pwandmw@blueyonder.co.uk